# The Reduced History of

# CATS

First published in 2007 by
André Deutsch Ltd
An imprint of the
Carlton Publishing Group
www.carltonpublishing.co.uk

Copyright © André Deutsch Ltd 2007

A CIP catalogue record for this book is available from the
British Library

ISBN: 978-0-233-00196-8

Printed in Singapore

Commissioning Editor: Martin Corteel
Project Art Editor: Darren Jordan
Production: Lisa French

# The
# Reduced History of
# CATS

## The story of our feline companion
## in 101 caterwauling episodes

Richard Pendleton Illustrations by Tony Husband

ANDRE
DEUTSCH

**Other titles in the Reduced History series**

The Reduced History of Dogs

The Reduced History of Sex

The Reduced History of Britain

The Reduced History of Football

The Reduced History of Cricket

The Reduced History of Golf

The Reduced History of Rugby

The Reduced History of Tennis

# INTRODUCTION

Cats. We lavish affection on them, give them names that would disgrace the most aristocratic child and spend fortunes on giving them food that looks like the aftermath of an industrial accident. But what do we really know about an animal that came down from the trees 65 million years ago, into our homes 8,000 years ago, and was sick in someone's shoes just a few minutes later?

In this book, we seek to answer some of the pressing questions that cat owners ask. Well, some cat owners, anyway. If you've ever wondered what to do when your cat develops a persistent cough, why it purrs or why it always uses its tray just after you've cleaned it, then this book is of no interest.

If, however, you want to know what happened to the cat who went up a tree and never came down, how cats won a war and what happened when a vaudeville act asked "Do you want to see my pussy?" then you're in the right place, because we've replaced all the dull, useful things you need to know about cats with some much more entertaining ones.

The result is *The Reduced History of Cats*. Like the animals themselves, it's fabulously irrelevant, but very engaging.

# LETTING THE CAT OUT OF THE BAG

# Tree historic feline

Arboreal ancestor of all cats decides to branch out

Sixty-five million years ago, the dinosaurs were wiped out. Survival was no longer a matter of having a huge body and a brain the size of a walnut. Up in the trees, furry, twitching things with whiskers realized their time had come.

Fast forward 30 million years, and one of the furry, twitching things had evolved into the first true cat, known to science as Proailurus. Slightly bigger than today's domestic cat, Proailurus looked a lot like a weasel, but not for long.

Evolution picked up speed, and the cat family tree later split into sabre-toothed tigers, and what became the Felidae family, containing every type of modern cat from the most potent panther to the most minuscule moggy.

The sabre-toothed tigers went the way of the dinosaurs, but the Felidae family has prowled on, an evolutionary victory for fur and guile over bulk and brawn.

Not all of the early versions of the cat were a success.

# 2 Heavenly petting

Virtue is its own reward for celestial cat

Everyone has made bets that they later regret, but according to one Hindu story two visitors to the court of Salamgam, King of the Indies, made a claim so lavish that it eclipsed even the most ambitious boasts of multiple beer-mat-flipping.

The argument was over who was the most virtuous, and it was won by the owner of a cat called Patripatan, who proved his virtue by sending the cat to pick a flower from the Parisadam tree, which grows only in heaven.

Unfortunately, a goddess fell in love with the beautiful Patripatan, and kept her for 300 years. Fortunately, everyone stayed young while they waited, and Patripatan finally returned with a whole branch of the Parisadam tree, but if you've ever spent hours waiting for your cat to come in, you'll know exactly how her owner felt.

# Miaow und Drang

Valhalla resounds to the drum of mighty paws

The gods and goddesses of Norse mythology were famously ferocious. Most were never happier than when they were having epic battles while wearing very severe headgear. But some had a gentler side, like Freya,

goddess of love, fertility and beauty, who had a mighty chariot – pulled by cats.

Yes, that's right. Cats. You might think that an animal that wakes up only to eat, chase toys around in a desultory fashion and then

Freya began to have doubts about her choice of transport.

vigorously wash its bottom would be out of place in a turbulent world of on-demand storms and mighty tales of derring-do, but these were very special cats indeed.

Freya, whose long flaxen hair would shame a shampoo advert, and who cried tears of gold, was clearly not the kind of girl who would be satisfied with two mangy relics from the Oslo branch of the RSPCA. Instead, her two cats were said to be the size of lions.

A present from Thor, the god of thunder, the cats were said to be blue-grey and to be the forebears of the modern-day breed known as the Norwegian Forest Cat. Legend doesn't reveal what the cats were fed on, but it's probably safe to assume that it included some kind of mushroom, as the chariot they pulled is often depicted flying across the heavens.

The legend omitted one important detail. What happens to the people on the ground when two strapping, well-fed cats pulling a flying chariot need to use the litter tray...?

**First of the divine felines**

Bast lives life at the apex of the cat pyramid

Having the head of a cat on the body of a woman might sound like less of a sign of divinity than of a rogue scientist run amok, but it's this very same form that the Egyptian goddess Bast was believed to inhabit.

Bast was revered as the lion-like guardian of Lower Egypt, but must have devoted more time to napping and chasing small balls of yarn as Lower Egypt was later conquered by Upper Egypt. Bast duly went through an early form of makeover which saw her becoming much closer to the domestic cat, but she was still worshipped as one of the more fierce Egyptian gods.

Her function was as a protector, mainly of the pharaoh, but also of women and children, and she was often invoked as a fertility symbol. But Bast has recently been reinvented in more plausible form in Terry Pratchett's Discworld series as "The God of Things Left on the Doorstep or Half-Digested Under the Bed".

# 5 Doing the leonine snuffle

Sneezing lion that brought forth a species

Not everybody thinks that cats evolved over millions of years. An alternative version has it that they were created in order to satisfy a particular pest control problem on the Ark.

Not all of the animals who had filed in two by two can have had their minds on higher things, as the rodents' over-enthusiastic breeding soon began to cause problems for Noah and family, so Noah offered up a prayer for help with the rampant rodents, and God replied by causing the lion to sneeze.

The crew might have expected to have been sprayed with several litres of lion phlegm, but instead two cats shot out of the lion's nose and landed on the deck. Their mousing abilities solved Noah's problem, while the cat-sneezing lion had provided history with the first and most literal case of cat flu.

Has anyone seen the mice recently?

# Desert cats

Cambyses gets catty as Egyptians fight shy

Egypt, 525 BC. Facing a difficult away fixture against the Egyptian army, Cambyses, the Persian ruler, decided to adopt imaginative new tactics.

Cambyses needed to take the Egyptian city of Pelusium, but instead of laying siege to it, he used the fact that Egyptians worshipped cats and other animals to his own advantage by placing them in front of his troops.

The cats' reaction is lost in the mists of time, as is the explanation of how long it took the Persians to get the cats to march, but Cambyses' tactics had the desired effect. Faced with the choice between wiping out their entire belief system in an afternoon's hard fighting, or giving up the city, they gave up the city.

Pelusium fell without so much as a "miaow" being uttered in anger and the Persians conquered Egypt, leaving the Egyptians wishing that they worshipped something less cute, less furry and altogether much easier to throw spears at.

The Egyptians fell for it every time.

# 7 Moggies sans frontières

Travelling cats exploit their right to Rome

It came, it saw, it slept.

"I came, I saw, I conquered," said Julius Caesar in a moment of typical modesty, but what the Roman leader failed to notice was that he was being manipulated by a conspiracy of cats.

For centuries, cats had been confined to ancient Egypt, so valued for their skills at keeping ancient Egyptian mice away from the ancient Egyptian grain that exporting them was banned. Some stole away across the Mediterranean, but it was the spread of the Roman Empire that got cats going places.

The Romans put cats to work wherever troops were stationed, and as Europe resounded to the measured tread of sandals and the swish of togas, cats treated the Romans as their own export business.

Within a few hundred years, cats had quietly spread across Europe, and outlasted the Romans who had brought them there. As the Roman Empire fell, cats yawned, and smugly said to themselves: "We came, we saw, we slept."

# 8 The feline creed

Dogma no match for cats with faith

The ancient Egyptians saw cats as gods in their own right, but they've also found a place in many other religions.

When the Prophet Muhammad found that his tabby, Muezza, had gone to sleep on the sleeve of his robe, he cut away the sleeve rather than disturb the sleeping cat. The rule of "if I sleep on it, it's mine" is now firmly established, but Muhammad may have left the cat another legacy.

The distinctive "M" marking on the forehead of all tabby cats is said to have been created when the Prophet placed his hand on Muezza's head. A Christian version of the same story says that the "M" stands for "Madonna" and appeared after the purring of a tabby kitten helped send the baby Jesus to sleep.

Tabbies remain quiet on the subject. Like all cats, they're happy to accept adoration from everyone.

# 9 The noun's the thing

From kadis to cattus and into the lexicon

There's something satisfying about the word "cat", but like cats themselves the word took several generations to evolve.

Linguistic boffins with too much time on their hands have worked out that the word began with the Nubians and the Berbers, who lived in different parts of Africa. While the Nubians were referring to the thing with four paws and a tail, and which kept turning up demanding food, as kadis, the Berbers had decided to call it kadiska.

As cats began to travel across the Mediterranean, the different words travelled with them. Kadis and kadiska became cattus in Latin and, as Latin spread across Europe, cattus was corrupted as Europeans translated it into their own languages.

By the seventh century, it had become "cat", and owners breathed a sigh of relief. After all, shouting "that bloody Felis cattus has done something in my shoe" just doesn't sound quite right.

# 10 Missing lynx
Bakanga, Ikimizi and Bung-Bung cause a rumble in the jungle

"We may be in trouble."

Each region of Africa seems to have its own psychopathic killer cat, never happier than when it's dragging off a luckless tribesman. The Central African Republic has the Bakanga, Rwanda has the Ikimizi and Cameroon has the Bung-Bung, but the most well-documented is the Mngwa.

Stories of this donkey-sized cat with grey striped fur were regarded by British settlers in Tanzania as quaint local folklore, until some horrific maulings during the 1920s led to Mngwa being taken much more seriously.

Mustachioed hunters ventured forth over the years, hoping to bag the Mngwa. They all failed, but they discovered a set of outsized tracks that gave some substance to the legend.

Some people believe that the Mngwa is a rare new species, others that it may just be a known species with different colouring, but if you're brave enough to find out yourself, you'll need a lot of cat food – and a very big net.

# Jailhouse cats

Cats of conviction bend the rules

If a small, tousled-haired child fell down a well, you could bank on good old Lassie to turn up, fetch Jeff, and help haul him out. But history records the stories of two cats whose efforts made Lassie's weekly well rescues look pedestrian.

When the Earl of Southampton was imprisoned in the Tower of London in the early seventeenth century, his intrepid cat, Trixie, defied adversity and a slightly twee name to find him and join him in his cell.

Sir Henry Wyatt was imprisoned in the Tower of London in 1483, and was kept alive by an even more resourceful but nameless cat that brought him a fresh pigeon every day and kept him warm at night.

Both prisoners survived to be released. Trixie was immortalized in a painting commissioned by her owner, and rumour has it that the ghost of Wyatt's cat haunts a church – presumably looking for anyone who fancies a nice bit of freshly mauled pigeon.

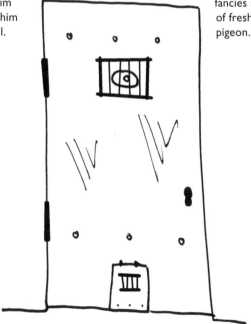

# Cauldron of hate

Ill-advised persecution leaves bigots feeling sore

The jury were unable to reach a verdict.

Cats went from divine to demonic in a few generations, perhaps because they were linked with the religious rites of the ancient world, but whatever the reason the belief soon took hold that they were used in witchcraft.

By the Middle Ages, thousands of cats were being killed and subjected to cruel treatment by people who believed that they were allies of the Devil. Not only was this attitude to cats barbaric, it also turned out to have some dramatic consequences for the people doing the persecuting.

Europe was decimated by the plague, carried, as it turned out, by fleas living on the very rat population which the cats had helped to control. The bad news for Europe was that nobody ever

made a link between the lack of cats, the sudden growth in the number of rats and the equally large numbers of people dying an agonizing death while covered in pustulant sores.

Pope Innocent VIII, a splendid humanitarian who was also a zealous supporter of the Spanish Inquisition, gave official approval to the persecution in 1484 with the witless pronouncement that witches not only worshipped Satan, but that they also took on the form of animals, including cats.

In England, the death penalty for witchcraft was finally abolished in 1736, by which time cats' rehabilitation was already well under way, but it was too late for 34 million Europeans. Cats, as always, had had the last laugh.

# European monks' cats go America

New World supine as cats take missionary position

Nobody is quite sure when cats arrived in North America. Some say that they first sauntered over with the Vikings, but others reckon they were introduced when Jesuit missionaries arrived in the seventeenth century. What is certain is that, once they'd got there, they didn't waste time making themselves at home.

The Jesuits were keen to convert the New World to the faith, and were so sure of their ability to educate people in the ways of the Church that their favourite maxim was "Give me a child for his first seven years, and I will give you the man." But even their zeal paled in comparison to their cats' appetite for expansion.

Four hundred years later, it's estimated that there are around 100 million domestic and feral cats in the USA alone. The Jesuits had given the cats a lift to the New World, and the cats had given them a continent. Full of other cats.

# A CAT ALWAYS LANDS ON ITS FEET

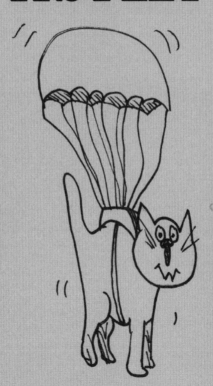

# Dick Whittington had a cat? Oh no he didn't...

Capital story of a fictional mayoral cat marches off into history

Behind every great man, they say, is a great woman. If the camera panned back a bit, they might also notice that getting under the great man's feet, leaving regurgitated biscuits in the great man's shoes and shedding hair on all of the great man's clothes, is a great cat.

Dick Whittington was just such a great man. The youngest son of Sir William Whittington, he travelled to London after his older brother inherited the family estate on their father's death in 1538. Whittington made his fortune as a cloth merchant, and later served four terms of office as Lord Mayor, becoming known for his generosity towards a wide range of good causes.

Looking for reasons as to why Whittington could have become so wealthy, Londoners quickly got to work inventing stories about where his money could have come from and, despite their mayor being conspicuously cat-less for all of his career, they decided that he owed it all to a fictitious feline.

Whittington was supposed to have sold the cat, a champion mouser, to the king. Why the king would spend millions on a cat when he could have got one from the Cats' Protection League for the price of a few tins of Whiskas was never fully explained, and nor was the name of the cat, but it passed into popular legend.

The story proved so popular that it became the basis for a pantomime which has cheered generations of dads at Christmas time by having Whittington played by a perky young actress in fishnet tights.

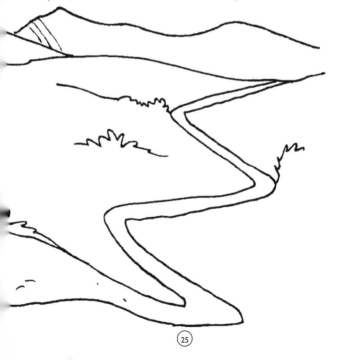

# 15 Lives insurance

Mortality beckons but cats say "nine"

Exactly why they're thought to have eight more lives than everything else that walks, swims and scuttles may never be known, but it probably became part of cat folklore at some point in the late sixteenth century.

It could be something to do with cats' capacity for getting into and then out of danger with consummate skill, but the fascination with the number nine is easier to explain. Three was often seen as a lucky number because of its associations with the Holy Trinity, so nine, a trinity of trinities, would be even more lucky.

Whatever the explanation, cats aren't complaining, least of all Mina, a black kitten who crawled into the engine compartment of a car for a nap in June 2005, and survived a 30-mile trip to Matlock, where she was finally rescued. Shaken, stirred and a bit greasy, Mina's first action was to eat her rescuer's pork pie.

# 16 Greying Matilda
Nostradamus' cat waltzes back to the future

In the sixteenth century, "Grimalkin" was the generic name for an old female cat, combining the word "grey" with "malkin", a slang term for the name Matilda, and the most famous of them all was the Grimalkin who belonged to an astrologer called Michel de Nôtre-Dame, better known as Nostradamus.

Nostradamus was famous for his predictions, and it's said that he predicted the rise of Hitler, although what he actually predicted was the rise of Hister – so he was probably referring to the rise of the Danube, known to the ancient Greeks as Ister.

Still, his talent must have come in very handy for knowing when Grimalkin would want to go out, or when he would need to go up to Le Tesco and buy some new cat litter.

**Four paws in a land down under**

Cats win residency as toads get caned

Cats probably arrived in Australia with the first traders some time in the seventeenth century, but only got down to some serious colonizing in the 1890s, when they were introduced to control the country's burgeoning rabbit population.

They soon proved to be a bigger problem than the rabbits had ever been, and were declared to be vermin, but just to show they hadn't learned any lessons, the Australian authorities made the same mistake again a few years later by introducing cane toads to eat the cane beetles.

The toads wrought havoc with the native wildlife by eating it and are now being exterminated, while Australia's cat population watch from a safe distance, happy to nap while the toads take the rap.

# 18 A local cat for unearthly people

The mysterious Rutterkin departs Rutland under a sulphurous cloud

"There's a large cat at the door, says he wants a word."

The stories that linked cats with witchcraft were just fearful rumours, but if you're going to scare people, you may as well do it properly. Like Rutterkin.

Rutterkin belonged to a Mistress Joan Flower, who worked, along with her daughters, for the Earl of Rutland. Flower was described as "full of oaths, curses, and imprecations irreligious", while her daughters were said to have been unruly. By 1618, the earl had heard an irreligious imprecation too many and sacked them.

Flower allegedly used Rutterkin's unearthly powers to curse Rutland and his family. He must have been quite a cat, as the earl's son died, his other children fell ill and the couple became infertile.

After Joan Flower died in prison, her daughters confessed to crimes so lewd and grotesque that they would have been deemed too unrealistic to make into a Hammer horror film. They were executed, but as to the whereabouts of Rutterkin? Nobody knows…

# The cat wore Prada

Handsomely shod feline tramples his way to the top

It's hard to think of a more surreal story than *Puss in Boots*, the account of how an upwardly mobile cat with an avant-garde taste in footwear masterminds his owner's ascent of the social ladder and then tops it off by eating an ogre who had turned himself into a mouse.

A number of details are left unexplained, not least why nobody was surprised by a talking cat, why he wore boots or how he managed to put them on without

opposable thumbs. But since it first appeared in 1634, the story has been retold in various forms and become a classic.

It tells the story of a miller's son who is left with nothing but the granary cat after his father's death. The cat wins his master favour with the king by giving him some game on his behalf. He also persuades the king to visit his master's palace, which belongs to a local ogre.

Persuading the unusually credulous ogre to turn into a mouse, the cat catches and then eats him, claiming the lands and palace for his master. Suitably impressed, the king's daughter marries the miller's son, and both he and the cat live a life of affluence and ease.

The story was one of a number written up by the French writer Charles Perrault for *Mother Goose Tales*, a collection published in 1697 that established the fairy tale genre. Many had a moral, although the main lesson from *Puss* seems to be that guile will always win the day. And having a talking cat won't do you any harm, either.

Isaac Newton supposedly discovered the principles of gravity after being hit by a falling apple. The story was probably made up by his PR people, but as well as dodging fictional fruit the cat-loving scientist is also credited with that most important of inventions – the cat flap.

This story probably has no more substance than the one about the apple, but it's said that Newton invented the cat flap to stop his cat from interrupting his work by mewing when she wanted to go out. When the cat had kittens, he made a smaller door for them as well.

A more prosaic explanation is that Newton kicked the door in frustration after finding that the cat was on the wrong side of it for the 50th time that morning. Deciding to make a virtue out of necessity by turning the dent into the world's first cat flap, he did for joinery what he'd already done for gravity.

The history of gravity, part one.

# Surplice to requirements

All cats welcome in cardinal's feline flock

Cardinal Richelieu had an unfortunate reputation. Known to historians as an enthusiastic persecutor of witches and to filmgoers as an equally enthusiastic persecutor of the Three Musketeers, he left behind a surprising legacy when he died in 1642. Cats. Lots and lots of cats.

The cardinal may not have been a moderate theologian, but it turns out that he was liberal, not to say indulgent, when it came to cats, and had 14 of them.

Making the most of their position at the top of the ecclesiastical food chain, the cats slept on the cardinal's bed and even had their own room next to his. It suggests that even Richelieu had a lighter side, and maybe even a sense of irony.

One of his cats was called Lucifer, which also happens to be the name of the archangel cast out of heaven – better known as Satan.

# **22** Paw performance
Strolling cat still strikes the right note

After Charles M. Schulz.

Domenico Scarlatti was an Italian composer best remembered for creating a huge number of sonatas, and for a fugue that celebrated his cat Pulcinella's habit of walking up and down the keyboard of his harpsichord.

Far from being the kind of cat who would scamper up and down for five minutes and pass the resulting racket off as free-form jazz, Pulcinella almost seemed to be picking out tunes.

Suitably inspired, the maestro scribbled down the results of one of these strolls, and Pulcinella's dextrous paws passed into history as "The Cat's Fugue". Scarlatti died in 1757, but has had a lasting influence on music written for the keyboard, and earned the lasting admiration of cats everywhere, who can claim that they're not attention-seeking, they're just being creative.

# Maine Coon, not a racoon

Freezing winters no obstacle to hirsute hybrid

Anyone with a basic knowledge of reproductive biology would be able to tell you that an attempt to breed a racoon with a cat would result in an embarrassed cat and an offended racoon, but this bizarre theory may explain how the breed of cat known as the Maine Coon got its name – if not its distinctive characteristics.

The cat's bushy tail and wide eyes probably gave the theory extra credence, but a much less biologically awkward explanation is that, once upon a time, an ordinary short-haired domestic cat met up with a long-haired cat, and the result was a hybrid whose thick coat and extra-furry paws left it well placed to survive the harsh New England winters.

The Maine Coon's gentle nature makes it a popular pet, and its handsome features make it an ideal show cat, but if you happen to own a cat and a racoon, it's probably best just to leave them to their own devices.

# 24 Mr Lover Cat

Tom makes a name as a lewd Lothario

It's not often someone changes the English language, and even less often that that person happens to be a fictional cat, but the publication of *The Life and Adventures of a Cat* in 1760 saw the name of the eponymous feline hero enter the lexicon as the name of all male cats – Tom.

The book may have been inspired by Fielding's *The History of Tom Jones*, a bawdy, bacchanalian brawl through the bedrooms of England, published in 1749, but whatever the explanation, Tom the cat's heroic devotion to his carnal duties more than matched that of his human counterpart.

Tom had clearly made an impression on the reading public. Male cats would no longer be known as "ram cats", but, following Tom's example, would still be just as horny.

# A CAT HAS
# NINE LIVES

# 25 The definitive cat

Hodge becomes the leading light of feline study

DR JOHNSON

Dr Johnson was a literary colossus in every sense. As well as looking uncannily like a man who existed on an all-pie diet, he wrote works of biography and criticism, of poetry and prose, and spent nine years working on what would become his greatest achievement – his *Dictionary of the English Language*.

He even appeared in *Blackadder* (although it's unlikely that he'd have enjoyed being referred to as Dr Fatty Know-It-All), and was followed around slavishly by his adoring biographer, James Boswell. It's from Boswell's equally weighty *Life of Johnson* that we know about Hodge, arguably literature's most literary cat. Johnson fed Hodge on oysters

he bought himself, fearing that his servants would resent the cat if they had to take time out from their normal duties to buy its food. Boswell was surprised by the indulgent way that Johnson treated Hodge, but maybe he just wanted to sit on the great man's knee as well.

When Hodge was in his final hours, Dr Johnson is said to have found some valerian, a herb used as a sedative, to soothe him, and the poet Percival Stockdale wrote "An Elegy on the Death of Dr Johnson's Favourite Cat" to mark his passing.

Johnson died in 1784, and his house in Gough Square, in London, is now a museum. A bronze statue of Hodge sitting on Johnson's dictionary was unveiled outside the house in 1997, summing up literary cats' admirable lack of pretension. To their owners, it's a life's work. To the cat, it's a comfy seat.

# Trim sails and hauls anchor

Antipodean adventurer who charted the course of history

Many marine moggies have ventured far from their sunny windowsills to seek out new lands and ever-bigger fish, but it all came naturally to Matthew Flinders' cat, Trim.

Trim was born at sea on HMS *Reliance* during a trip to Cape Town in 1797. The black and white cat endeared himself to Captain Flinders, and the two became firm friends. He joined Flinders for the voyages on which he mapped the coast of Australia, and they became the first man and the first cat to circumnavigate the continent.

Flinders and Trim had to stop off at Mauritius on the way home, where Flinders was imprisoned by the French, who suspected him of spying. Trim died on the island, but in 1996 he was given his own statue, just behind the statue of Flinders that stands outside the Mitchell Library in Sydney. It took nearly 200 years, but Trim is finally standing on dry land.

# Poetic mews

Keats honours cats in words and deeds

John Keats was just 25 years old when he died in 1821, but he left behind some of the greatest poetry in the English language, including one of the most famous cat poems, titled "To Mrs Reynolds' Cat".

An unlikely celebration of an elderly, asthmatic cat that wheezed, it describes the cat's eyes as "bright languid segments green", which is worth a few shillings of anyone's money.

Unusually for a poet given to ennui, doomed love affairs and tuberculosis, Keats was a ready defender of his furry brethren, and was remarkably handy with his fists, which turned out to be very bad news for a butcher's boy whom he caught tormenting a kitten.

"Ode upon Battering the Butcher's Boy" would have been a welcome addition to the Keats' canon, but for his proactive stance on animal cruelty – and for "To Mrs Reynolds' Cat", we salute him.

# Reigning queen protects cats

Animal charity given royal seal of approval

1840 was a landmark moment in the history of cats' welfare. It was not the year of the first can-opener, or of the self-emptying litter tray, but the regal seal of approval from Queen Victoria that saw the Society for the Prevention of Cruelty to Animals add the word "Royal" to its name.

The RSPCA, as it became known, was founded in London way back in 1824 by 22 people concerned about the plight of animals. One of the founders, an MP called Richard Martin, had already helped to steer the first legislation against animal cruelty through Parliament, and the Society's uniformed volunteers acted as a law-enforcement organization that pre-dated the formation of a national police force by five years.

Today it costs £82 million to meet the charity's annual running costs, and it receives no government funding, so when you've finished reading this book, why not stick your paw in your pocket and make a donation?

# 29 King leer

Unsettling cat grins its way into literary history

The first edition of Lewis Carroll's *Alice's Adventures in Wonderland* was published in 1865 to give people something to read during the long wait for the invention of LSD. It ushered many characters into the pantheon of children's fiction, none of them more disturbing than the Cheshire Cat.

It's not known what gave Carroll the inspiration for the cat, a feline that disappears until all that is left is a maniacal grin. Some suggest that it was a legend of a swordsman from Cheshire who grinned as he saw off his adversaries, others that it was a gargoyle in the church where Carroll's father was rector – or maybe Cheshire cheeses made in the shape of grinning cats.

Nobody knows for sure, although the possibility that it was due to smoking some of whatever it was that was in the toadstool-dwelling caterpillar's hookah pipe has to be a strong contender. In the words of the cat, "We're all mad here."

Well, quite. Smoke one for me, Lewis C.

Post Office cats took their job very seriously.

Nothing upsets a postman more than finding out that his mail has been nibbled in the night by an errant rodent, which is perhaps why the Post Office decided to recruit the first official post office cats in 1868.

The first three were given a trial at the Money Order Office in London. In the first recorded instance of performance-related pay, the cats received a shilling a week, but still had to catch mice to avoid going hungry. It turned out to be a success, and more cats were employed at other post offices across the country.

Plastic, rodent-resistant sacks heralded the slow decline of the post office cat, but the most famous of all is still going strong – Postman Pat's cat, Jess, has now been given his own show, "Guess with Jess".

[with thanks to the Postal Heritage Trust]

# Land of the rising paw

Porno past of Japan's perkiest pets

Along with the neon lights of Tokyo, the distinctive architecture and vast armies of teenage girls obsessed with David Beckham, one of the iconic images of Japanese culture is the cat known as a Maneki Neko.

Japanese for "Beckoning Cat", Maneki Neko is the name of the stylized figurines showing plump cats sat on their haunches with one of their front paws raised. They became popular in late-nineteenth-century Japan with merchants who saw them as good luck symbols, enticing customers into their shops.

The raised left paw encourages custom, but Maneki Neko can now be seen with raised right paws, said to bring wealth. The higher the paw, the luckier the cat, although not everyone who displays present-day Maneki Neko may be aware of the alternative explanation behind their early popularity.

According to the website manekinekoclub.com, Japanese brothels began using them to represent a coyly welcoming prostitute after their more traditional display of wooden phallic symbols was made illegal in 1872.

# Fancy hats and fancier cats

First cat show a feast of Victorian vanity

Every cat owner is proud of their cat, and believes that they possess special qualities which set them above the average moggy. In 1871, they were given the opportunity to put this to the test when the first official cat show was held at Crystal Palace.

Organized by writer and artist Harrison Weir, known to posterity by the slightly unfortunate title "the father of cat fancy", who also acted as one of the judges, the show attracted 170 entrants and a surprisingly large crowd.

The field was divided up into several different categories (no pun intended) and included a cat from Scotland with only three paws. The prize for biggest in show went to a brown tabby who belonged to one Miss Amos, while the inaugural award for best in show was given to a British blue short-hair, who just happened to be owned by Mr Weir. Fancy that.

# 33 **Catalogue of brutality**
Unwelcome strokes of a feline feared by all

The other cat o'nine tails.

Of all the ships' cats that served in the Royal Navy, there was one whose reputation was so fearsome that it could strike fear into the heart of the most seasoned sailor, and in 1881 crews everywhere must have cheered when they heard news of its retirement. Its name? The cat o'nine tails.

The cat was also known as "The Captain's Daughter", presumably because it was at his command, and not because the sailors felt a similar dislike for the Alexander Pushkin novel of the same name. Its "tails" were nine pieces of rope attached to a baton, and one explanation for the origin of the phrase "let the cat out of the bag" is that the "cat" was kept in a canvas bag when it wasn't being used.

Changing attitudes brought flogging to an end by 1881, and marked the demise of the one cat that was never welcome on board.

# Bones of contention

Archaeology a mixed blessing for mummified moggies

It's better not to think too deeply about where fertilizer comes from, but it would have been especially unwise if you were a nineteenth-century cat lover.

In 1888 a farmer in Beni Hassan in Egypt discovered an underground vault that contained the mummified remains of thousands of cats, preserved for posterity by the feline-worshipping ancient Egyptians. Or so they thought.

Where some people saw a cat necropolis that could yield valuable insights into the place of the cat in Egyptian culture and mummification processes, others saw a major business opportunity. The mummies were duly broken up and the bones of around 80,000 cats were shipped to Manchester to be ground up for fertilizer.

# Oh, pussy my love

Salacious sisters get cat calls for baring nearly all

The jaded reaction that saw Madonna's snog with Britney at the MTV Awards in 2003 dubbed as a doomed attempt to generate some sales-friendly controversy showed just how hard it is to shock modern audiences. But back in the 1890s the Barrison Sisters stunned the world by asking: "Do you want to see my pussy?"

The Danish-American sisters were a vaudeville act, knowingly advertised as being "the wickedest girls in the world" to lure in paying punters, and were already known for spicy double entendres before they premiered their most risqué routine.

After posing the question "Do you want to see my pussy?" to the men of the audience who were already mad with lust – and, this being the 1890s, curiosity – they duly raised their skirts to reveal that the pussies in question were, in fact, real live kittens peeking out of the crotch of their bloomers.

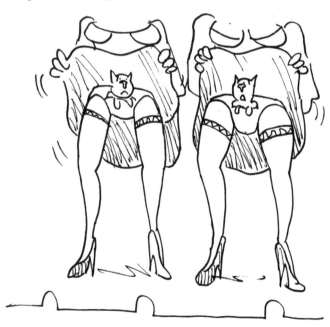

It was either this or panto again.

# Birman: aristocat in exile
## Stone temple cats make a break for freedom

With its golden fur, smoky brown face and serene, soulful eyes, the Birman is an exotic and aristocratic cat, and, as with all aristocrats in exile, there has been endless speculation and intrigue as to its true background.

Legend has it that a Khmer priest was killed by robbers, and as the white cat who had been his companion in his prayers lay its paws on him, its fur become golden and its eyes became blue.

Days later a hundred cats carried his soul to paradise, but how Birmans reached Europe is even more of a mystery.

Some say that a pair was given to Major Gordon Russell and his friend Auguste Pavie as a reward for protecting a Khmer temple, others claim that a pair were stolen and given to a rich American.

As for the Birmans, they're far too discreet to say.

# 37 Catanory

Story-telling cat mocks occidental ways

In 1905, Japanese writer Natsume Soseki published a pungent satire on the Japanese middle class at the turn of the twentieth century, a time when Japan was beginning to experiment with more Western ways. Soseki is one of Japan's greatest novelists and his choice of the book's narrator was a stroke of genius.

*I am a Cat* is presented from the point of view of a cat, whose aloof and sarcastic observations show up the family's behaviour as trivial and silly. From thwarted cultural aspirations to status anxiety via nostril hair-plucking, the cat sees it all with the same mercilessly mocking eye.

The book began as a short story, but the combination of its cynical narrator and his creator's astute observations meant that the original story became the first of several chapters, and Soseki went on to become famous, a social leap that his feline narrator would almost certainly have had an opinion on…

Tom Kitten didn't really mind being sent to bed early.

In 1907, Beatrix Potter published *The Tale of Tom Kitten*, the story of three kittens who get dirty, get into an argument with some ducks and who are then sent upstairs early to have a bit of a think about what they've done.

Her books might not have been searing critiques of contemporary society, but they were beautifully illustrated, lovingly told and gave their author her own income at a time when women were expected to be doe-eyed, timid creatures who delegated tricky things like thinking and opinions to their husbands.

Potter's attempt to study at the Royal Botanical Gardens in Kew was thwarted because she was female, so her animal stories became an important outlet.

And if, like this author, you remember eating your earliest meals off a Peter Rabbit plate, her drawings have a grace, charm and hold on the emotions that are the very stuff of childhood. Hoorah for Tom Kitten and chums, we say.

# Tail of endurance

Mrs Chippy stands on the shoulder of a carpentry giant

In 1914, Mrs Chippy won a small, cat-sized place in history as the feline mascot of the *Endurance*, the ship that carried Ernest Shackleton on the Imperial Trans-Arctic expedition.

Mrs Chippy was in the care of Harry "Chippy" McNeish, the expedition's carpenter, and despite the name was a male cat, whose favourite pastime was taunting the sled dogs by leaping over their kennels. But when the *Endurance* found itself trapped in sea ice, Shackleton shot Mrs Chippy and all the dogs to save rations.

A rescue mission later succeeded, but Shackleton spitefully denied the award of the Polar Medal to McNeish, who had quarrelled with him. In 2004 a life-size bronze statue of Mrs Chippy was unveiled on McNeish's grave, reuniting the pair after nearly a century. And as McNeish's grandson said to a BBC reporter, "I think the cat was more important to him than the Polar Medal."

Back in the day when animal characters were wholesome and films were silent, the strange, flickering adventures of Felix the Cat rewrote the rules. The cat was still quiet, but after a false start under the name "Master Tom" he quickly became the first celluloid cartoon star.

Felix came from Pat Sullivan's studio, although it's often suggested that he was less the work of Sullivan than of cartoonist Otto Messmer who also drew the Felix strips and the series of Felix cartoons that the studio made in the 1920s.

The arrival of the talkies and the all-singing, all-dancing Mickey Mouse did for Felix's run of success, but the cat refused to lie down, and Messmer's apprentice, Joe Oriolo, gave Felix a new lease of life by remaking him for TV.

In the words of his theme song, written at the height of his popularity, Felix keeps on walking – and shows no sign of stopping.

# WHEN THE CAT'S AWAY THE MICE WILL PLAY

# Intercontinental windswept cats

Lucky stars shine as Twinkletoe and co. survive heavy weather

Captain John Alcock and Lieutenant Arthur Whitten-Brown became the first to complete a non-stop flight across the Atlantic on 14 June 1919. It had been a windy crossing for Brown, who had to climb out on to the wings to remove ice from the engines, but an even windier one for Lucky Jim.

Lucky Jim was one of the two toy black cats the pair took with them as mascots, and spent the flight tied to one of the supporting struts on the wing of the biplane bomber that Alcock and Brown had borrowed for the flight. His partner, Twinkletoe, secured a more comfortable berth inside Brown's flight suit.

Both Lucky Jim and Twinkletoe were black cats, and if ever a flight needed luck it was Alcock and Brown's. Hours after leaving St John's in Newfoundland, the two men and their two cats ran into the two types of weather that early aviators feared: ice and fog.

Ice seized up the engines, causing them to misfire and sending Brown out on to the wing. Brown was also the navigator, and had to keep the aircraft on a steady course as fog swirled around it, but with the redoubtable and experienced Alcock at the controls, the first transatlantic flight arrived at Clifden in Ireland just over 16 hours later.

The aircraft ended the flight in a slightly undignified way, nose down in a peat bog, but the crew were unhurt. They had survived howling gales, ice-encrusted engines, swirling fog and now a crash-landing, a testament to their flying skills – and, just maybe, to the lucky powers of Twinkletoe and Lucky Jim.

It took a while for the mascot to thaw out.

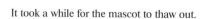

# A league of their own

Cats' Protection show that charity begins at the cats' home

Before 1927, cats had to protect themselves.

The RSPCA had already been doing sterling work to raise public awareness of the evils of animal cruelty, but in 1927 cats were given their very own charity when the Cats' Protection League was founded in London.

Its main concern was to educate people about the domestic cat, but the warm-hearted founders soon took a more hands-on approach to its work. By 1935, it had its first clinic, in a house in Slough, and during the war did its patriotic bit for Britain's bombed-out moggies when it launched "The Tailwavers' Scheme" to help cats in blitzed areas.

"Cats' Protection League" was shortened to "Cats' Protection" in 1998, presumably to avoid it being mistaken for a football tournament for rescued cats, and today it rescues and re-homes 60,000 cats a year. So whether you have a home to offer or want to help in other ways, there are a few thousand furry friends who will be glad of your support.

# Far from the funereal crowd

Faithful cat disappears after illustrious owner dies

Thomas Hardy died in 1928. He left behind a body of prose and poetry that explored the futility of man's endeavours in the face of remorseless fate with an eloquence and power that may as well be called genius. And a cat called Cobby.

It might be hard to imagine a writer who thwarted Jude, hanged Tess and broke Giles Winterbourne's heart treating his pets any better than his protagonists, but Hardy had been besotted with Cobby, a grey Persian he was given as a pet when he was in his final years.

The bond of devotion between the two was so strong that when the great writer died, Cobby disappeared as well. Depending on your opinion of cats, that could either indicate that Cobby was a wily old pragmatist who had sauntered off to find another owner, or that, like so many of Hardy's characters, he had walked into grief-stricken oblivion.

# Two luminous eyes

Flash of inspiration worth its weight in White Shield

On a dark, foggy night in 1933, Percy Shaw was driving home to Boothtown in Halifax along a road that fell away steeply on one side, with nothing but a flimsy fence between the road and a steep drop.

Percy could well have gone over the edge had his headlights not picked out the reflective eyes of a cat sitting on the fence. A year later, he took out the patent for a device that would have a lasting impact on road safety – roadstuds, better known as cats' eyes.

Or so the story goes. Yorkshiremen are not known for indulging in poetic flights of fancy and, when jet-setting TV journalist Alan Whicker made the journey up to Halifax many years later, the dour inventor had a much more prosaic explanation, and revealed that he had the idea after seeing reflectors on a road sign on his way home from the pub.

As one of 14 children, young Percy had been used to living by his wits and cats' eyes were merely one of a number of devices that the budding young inventor had come up with. But they proved to be the most successful.

The idea was brilliant in its simplicity, with small reflective pieces of glass in a raised rubber mat laid into the road surface that sank into a recess after being hit by a car, before springing back. In 1935 he started Reflecting Roadstuds Ltd to make them, and the company is still in business over 70 years later.

Percy earned enough from his invention to live comfortably for the rest of his life, but lived in Spartan seclusion. His sole concession to luxury was his two Rolls-Royces – and several crates of Worthington's White Shield beer.

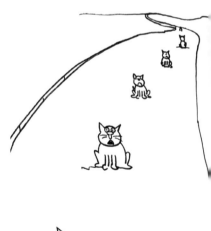

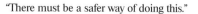

"There must be a safer way of doing this."

# 45 Quantum sleep

Schrödinger's cat naps as debate rages

The only thing more difficult than explaining the laws of quantum mechanics is demonstrating them. So in 1935, when the Austrian physicist Erwin Schrödinger devised a thought experiment to demonstrate a paradox of quantum mechanics, he had to seek help. From a hypothetical cat.

Schrödinger's experiment saw a notional cat being locked in a box with a canister of cyanide and a radioactive atom that has a 50% chance of decaying within an hour and triggering the release of the cyanide.

The paradox is that under the laws of quantum mechanics, the hypothetical atom has to be said to exist in a "superposition", neither decayed nor undecayed, until it can be observed – meaning that the cat is in the impossible position of being neither alive nor dead.

A more likely version features in Douglas Adams' *Dirk Gently's Holistic Detective Agency*, when it turns out that the box is empty and the bored cat has wandered off.

The cat's answer.

# Chariots of fur

Racing cats pull up short in pursuit of glory

Cats are not natural racing animals. Big cats might chase their prey out on the African plains, but domestic cats with a full bowl of food and a comfy chair just don't have the same motivation, which makes the decision to open a cat racing track look all the more bizarre.

The 200-metre track opened at Portisham in Dorset in 1936, and is said to have been similar to a greyhound track, albeit with the obligatory mangy rabbit replaced by an electric mouse.

No information exists as to who the first runners were and the chances are that the field found it all too demeaning and spent the race studiedly ignoring the mouse, sleeping, yawning or wandering off in the wrong direction.

Amazingly, the sport staggered on until the final meeting was held in 1949 and a short, ignoble chapter in the history of the cat was brought to a deserved end.

# 47 Old Possum discovers the joy of spandex

Smash hit musical sees unlikely pairing of impresario and dead poet

"I see that T. S. Eliot's ghost is in again."

In a radical departure, the poet T. S. Eliot, creator of *The Waste Land* and other highbrow poems, stunned the literary world by publishing *Old Possum's Book of Practical Cats*, in 1939, a move only slightly less unexpected than Hitler releasing a book on how to make comedy balloon animals.

*Old Possum* is a positively skittish and lighthearted – if typically erudite – look at the characters of different cats. Gone were the madmen shaking dead geraniums, the living dead who walked across London Bridge, and the troubling image of death as a smirking footman that made Eliot's earlier works such a cheery place to spend time, and in their stead was a much more jolly world.

This new world was peopled by Bustopher Jones the cat about town, the splendidly alliterative Magical Mr Mistoffelees and a range of other fabulously

BOO!

monickered moggies with names like Mungojerrie and Rumpleteazer which showed that, while Eliot might have been writing for an audience with an IQ half his own, he hadn't lost his love of word play.

His meditations on death and decay might have won him critical praise, but *Old Possum's Book of Practical Cats* is now Eliot's best-known work and gave him a strange new afterlife when it became the basis for the musical, *Cats*.

*Cats* sunk its claws in wherever it appeared, and showed about as much sign of letting go as a terrified tabby up a tree. It ran for ever. And ever. And ever – although the decision to remodel Eliot's determinedly quirky cats as lissom dancers in spandex was an act of revisionism that would have probably shocked even the dead geranium-shakers into sanity.

From cats in hats to cats in trousers, by way of cats playing golf, Louis Wain drew them all. He probably did more than any other artist to anthropomorphize cats and challenge negative attitudes to them, but by his death in 1939 he had created a very different series of cat pictures.

Wain suffered from late-onset schizophrenia, and one particular sequence of pictures is often used to illustrate the progress of the condition. The cats become more like cartoons, surrounded by jagged outlines in rainbows of colours until the outline is lost in a blaze of intricate patterns.

As fascinating as the pictures are, the illness that lay behind them cost Wain dearly. He was committed to the poor ward of a mental hospital in 1924. A national outcry saw him moved to more salubrious surroundings, although he never recovered. An artist who had become famous drawing for cats in hats, he left behind an unexpectedly fascinating legacy.

# Kinky Catwoman cracks the whip

Slinky who uses Bruce Wayne as her scratching post

Comics' most unashamedly kinky villain, Catwoman, aka Selina Kyle, made her debut in the *Batman* series of comic-books in 1940, later showing a love of revealing eveningwear and wearing a mask with little pointy ears that must have left her teenage readers with some very conflicting emotions.

Her memorable double entendre in *Batman* issue one – "I know when I'm licked" – may have been unintentional, but Kyle got more knowing and the outfits got more figure-hugging as the years went by, and with the addition of a whip to her arsenal, the transition from lady jewel thief to porno poster girl for budding sadomasochists was complete.

Catwoman has been reinvented by several different illustrators and even killed off a few times, but the sexual tension between her and Batman is a constant. Still, when two people given to hanging around at night dressed from head to toe in rubber meet, you'd expect them to have plenty to talk about.

Tracking down Catwoman proved to be remarkably easy.

# Tree's company

Mincha the cat opts for a life less earthbound

"And finally", says the newsreader, who, having regaled the viewing public with a litany of death and mayhem, changes to a gooey tone to introduce the heart-warming story of a cat who was stuck up a tree, but now isn't. Cats up trees are a reliable standby for the nightly news, unless their name happens to be Mincha.

Mincha was a black and white female cat that showed a shocking disregard for the news agenda by running up a 40-foot tree in Buenos Aires in 1948 and then staying there for years.

Locals fed her with food on poles and, instead of mewing herself hoarse, Mincha made good use of the time, as did the local tomcats. Mincha managed to get pregnant and give birth to several litters of kittens – all without leaving the tree.

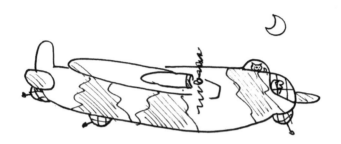

Wing Commander Guy Gibson is best known to animal lovers as the owner of the unfortunately-named Nigger, a black Labrador who was killed the day before the famous "Dam Busters" mission, but what's less widely known is that Gibson also owned a cat called Windy.

While Nigger reportedly flew on training missions with Gibson, legend has it that Windy went one better by accompanying him on operations. As Gibson was a bomber pilot at a time of the war when the RAF was using aircraft that belonged in a museum for flying deathtraps, Windy's survival in the face of flak and nightfighters was no mean achievement.

Gibson made "Nigger" the codeword for the breaching of the Mohne dam, a decision likely to cause a few problems for the scriptwriters working on the remake. If they surrender to political correctness and need to replace it, then maybe Windy will get his overdue 15 minutes of fame.

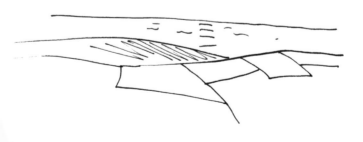

# Fortune favours the feline
Cat sails into history with Atlantic charter

"You're shorter than I remember, Mr Churchill."

1941 was a bleak year for Blighty. The country faced the might of Nazi Germany in noble isolation but, with U-boats prowling the north Atlantic and cutting off vital supplies, it was obvious to Churchill that outside help would be needed to keep Britain in the fight.

Churchill hoped that America, still a neutral country, might provide aid. He set up a meeting with President Roosevelt, sailing off to America on the battleship HMS *Prince of Wales*. Just as Churchill was about to disembark for his crucial meeting, the ship's cat suddenly turned up to wish him luck.

It must have worked. Roosevelt provided the necessary aid, and, with Churchill, drew up the document known as the "Atlantic Charter" which shaped the future of the post-war world. It also had a direct effect on the future of the ship's cat – it was renamed "Churchill".

# Unsinkable Sam floats on

Navy's most buoyant sailor bobs off into retirement

If being sunk once is a misfortune and being sunk twice looks like carelessness, then being sunk three times suggests that you should probably call time on your nautical career, which is exactly what happened to the cat known to feline naval history as Unsinkable Sam.

Sam started out as Oscar, the ship's cat of the fearsome German battleship *Bismarck*. The heavily armed *Bismarck* was bad news for Allied shipping and for the HMS *Hood*, which was sunk while giving chase, but the *Bismarck*'s luck ran out in May 1941 when she was crippled in a torpedo attack launched by planes from HMS *Ark Royal* and then pounded by destroyers and heavy cruisers.

*Bismarck* sank, taking over 2,000 of its crew with her, but not Oscar, who was picked up by HMS *Cossack*. Renamed Sam at some point in his time with the Royal Navy, he lasted just five months aboard his new ship before it was hit by a torpedo fired from a German U-boat and sunk in the Atlantic.

The crew were rescued by the HMS *Ark Royal*, the aircraft carrier whose planes had launched the attack which damaged the *Bismarck*, and Sam had another new ship. But not for long.

In November 1941, the *Ark Royal* was hit amidships by a single torpedo and soon began to list at an alarming angle. There was enough time to evacuate the entire crew – and Sam – before the carrier finally sank. Sam was picked up by HMS *Legion* which, perhaps reviewing his service history, thought better of it and saw him safely into retirement in England, where he lived out his days in peace.

HMS *Legion*'s fate, however, was grimly predictable. She sank a year later.

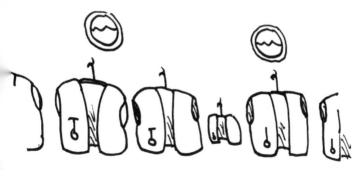

# Dark satanic cat

Brooding behemoth becomes a literary leviathan

Written by the Russian novelist Mikhail Bulgakov and completed by his wife after his death in 1941, *The Master and Margarita* is the story of what happens when Satan appears in downtown Moscow one sunny afternoon. Among his retinue is Behemoth, who stakes a claim to being literature's most disturbing cat.

Also spelled "Begemot", the name means "hippopotamus" in Russian and is a large Biblical beast, but the huge cat imagined by Bulgakov had distinctly demonic qualities.

A maniacal, chess-playing trickster with a dark sense of humour, he mercilessly persecutes the literary establishment, devises a series of

"amusements" for a demonic ball, and in his gory opening scene decapitates a man whose severed head is still able to talk.

Bulgakov buff Kevin Moss's website reveals that when one of the apartments which features in the book was visited in 1998, there was a black cat living there. His name? Begemot.

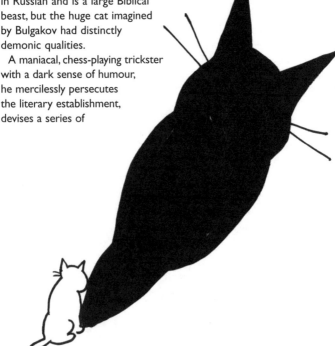

# 55 Kitty talk
Human speaks with feline tongue

Being trapped in a room with someone who insists that their cat can talk to them can be a disturbing experience, even for the most ardent cat lover, but it's just possible that the person who insists that she and Tibbles have the most fascinating little chats might have read Mildred Moelk's 1944 study.

Moelk argued that cats are able to make 16 different sounds by murmuring, trilling and closing their mouths as they "speak", with the sounds ranging from vowels to consonants and becoming more complex as the cat grows up.

The findings of Moelk's work were published as *Vocalizing in the House Cat*, published in the *American Journal of Psychology*, but more could have been made of the one sound that all cat owners dread – the terrible undulating moan that lets you know a hairball will soon be arriving on the bedroom carpet.

# Cat and mouse

Jasper and Jinx stay on drawing board as Tom and Jerry caper on

Tom and Jerry are the undisputed kings of cartoon comedy. They stormed to the title with a brand of cheery violence that saw an arsenal of domestic appliances being deployed in the slapstick spirit of silent films, and in 1946 they gave their finest performances.

The duo made their debut as Jasper and Jinx in a cartoon called *Puss Gets the Boot*. Released in 1940, it led to the pair being given their own series and with it a new name, thought up by animator John Carr in an in-house competition.

As Tom and Jerry, the staples of their brightly coloured universe became part of the comedy lexicon. Bulldogs wear spiked collars, every character's movement has a full orchestral accompaniment, including a strange, plinking piano noise as legs spin around in mid-air, and cute animals are seen doing unimaginable things to each other, but no injury is so severe that it can't be fixed by spending a few seconds out of shot.

*Cat Concerto* saw creators William Hanna and Joseph Barbera at the peak of their powers. Starting from the simple premise of Tom attempting to play a piano recital while Jerry attempts to stop him, the cartoon turns the piano into an instrument of carnage, all set seamlessly to Franz Liszt's Hungarian Rhapsody No. 2.

It did for classical music what being played with a chainsaw would do to a Stradivarius, but it won Tom and Jerry the fourth of their seven Academy Awards and is done with such antic glee that it becomes art in its own right.

OSCAR

# A CAT MAY
# LOOK AT A KING

# The cats who fell for earth

Inventor of cat litter gets the paws up from relieved customers

No cat owner's home is complete without the desert of dried turds known as the litter tray. This piece of performance art owes its existence to your cat and its zealous attention to its toilet duties, but also to Mr Edward Lowe, who invented cat litter in 1947.

Lowe carved out a career for himself in the thrusting world of industrial absorbents. After hearing that a neighbour who used ash in her cat's litter box was frustrated with the trail of grimy paw-prints, he gave her a type of clay known as Fuller's Earth to use instead.

The neighbour was delighted, paws were clean and Lowe had the basis for a new business. Naming his product "Kitty Litter", Lowe started by giving it away and then, when it proved popular, sold it in five-pound bags.

By 1990, his company had an annual turnover of $210 million, proving that where there's muck, there's brass.

Before cat litter.

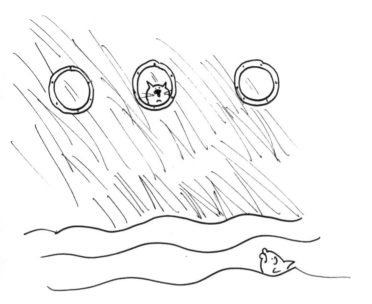

The Dickin Medal is animals' equivalent of the Victoria Cross. It's been awarded to Winkie, a plucky carrier pigeon, and to a dog that served with the SAS, and in 1949 it was awarded to its only feline recipient to date – Simon, the ship's cat of HMS *Amethyst*.

*Amethyst* was ordered to sail to Nanking in case people from the British Embassy needed to be evacuated as the communist revolution raged around them.

Britain was neutral, but communist shore batteries fired on the ship, killing some of the crew, and wounding others, including Simon. The little cat recovered, and raised morale by spending time with the wounded – and catching rats.

The plucky cat was nominated for the Dickin Medal, but, sadly, died back in Britain, before he could receive it. As befits such a stalwart, he was buried in a casket draped with the union flag – and his replacement had the best possible start to his career by being given the name Simon II.

# Felines are a girl's best friend

When men grow cold, Marilyn seeks solace in Mitsou

Marilyn Monroe was used, abused and generally patronized by most of her male companions, and offered up the poignant observation that "If you talk to a dog or a cat, it doesn't tell you to shut up", which may be why she had so many pets.

Cinema's most luminous star showed a marked preference for dogs, owning a black and white dog when she was young, a French poodle called Maf at the time of her death and a whole range of other mutts in between, but she did own a white Persian cat called Mitsou when she was living in New York.

Despite her famous owner, Mitsou is not a well-documented cat. We do know, however, that life became complicated when Marilyn tried to take her to the vet. "When I say 'This is Marilyn Monroe. My cat's having kittens'," she once said, "they think I'm some kind of nut and hang up."

# 60 Peak practice

Cat with wanderlust climbs the Matterhorn

In September 1950, a team of climbers who set out to tackle the Matterhorn were surprised when they were joined during the climb by a four-month-old kitten. They must have been even more surprised when the cat followed them all the way to the top of the mountain, a climb of 14,691 feet.

History doesn't record what the cat was doing on the mountain, especially as it belonged to one Josephine Aufdenblatten of Geneva, but the climbers were glad of the company, and gave it a lift back down in one of their rucksacks, naming it Cervinis, Italian for Matterhorn.

"Matterhorn" is currently used as the name of a certain type of indoor cat activity centre, although adventurous felines may feel disappointed when they find that their mountain has been reduced to some scratching posts and a ball on a string.

# Margate coasts home

Churchillian moggy inspires a bravura performance

Shortly before Churchill made a key speech in a seaside town in 1953, he took in a black and white stray cat. The speech was a success and Churchill duly named the cat after the town where it had been delivered. Thus "Margate" became the latest in a long line of Churchillian cats.

For someone often linked with talk of Britain as home of "the bulldog breed", an animal whose tenacious mien was a perfect match for the great man's doggedly defiant spirit during the dark years of the war, Churchill himself showed a marked fondness for cats.

He owned several during his two terms of office, including a black cat called Nelson after the famous admiral. Nelson kept him company during the Blitz and sat by him in the Cabinet room, but it's less certain that the Nazi hordes would have been deterred by hearing Britons described as "this tabby breed".

# Heat drives Vans to distraction

When temperatures rise, Turkish breed hits the water

Laura Lushington and Sonia Halliday might sound like catsuited crimefighters from a 1960s TV series, but they deserve a place in cat history as the ladies who rediscovered the Turkish Van cat breed in 1955.

Not, as it might sound, the product of an unfortunate collision between an unsuspecting cat and a speeding delivery vehicle from south-eastern Europe, the breed gets its name from Lake Van in Turkey. Turkish Vans had largely died out in Europe when Lushington and Halliday found them all over again during a trip through Turkey.

Vans are mainly white, with coloured heads and tails, but it's their behaviour that really sets them apart from other breeds – the Lake Van region gets very hot in summer, and the cats cool off by going for a swim, making them the world's only swimming vans.

# The first moggy of millinery

It's hat to the future in the weird world of Dr Seuss

Cat in a hat: the prototype.

Before 1957, the world of children's literature could often be a staid place full of earnest little chaps having horribly predictable conversations about trains or dogs called Timmy. And then it was all changed by an energetic feline. In a hat.

*The Cat in the Hat* was created by Theodore Geisel, better known under his pseudonym, Dr Seuss, after a book drew attention to poor literacy levels and linked the phenomenon with boring children's books. Geisel was asked to write a book to teach children 220 key words, with a cat in a hat to help them.

Seuss's ebullient cat, picked out with bold, curving lines, was a hit with children and in turn with parents, as dogs called Timmy and their drearily monosyllabic owners went back to the 1940s.

# 34 not out
Veteran cats pass a magic milestone

For a cat, reaching any age past 20 is classed as a good innings, but in 1957 a cat called Ma completed one innings, went back for a second and only retired to the pavilion after 34 years and a day.

Ma's longevity has been attributed variously to exposure to classical music as both her owners were musicians, to a ready supply of fresh meat or to the fact that she got her paw caught in a trap when she was a kitten and always received extra-zealous care.

Even after 50 years, Ma occupies her own place in feline history as still the oldest British cat, but the international title was claimed in 1998 by Granpa, from Texas, who was 34 years, two months and four hours old when he handed in his bowl, although both the cat's name and the fact his life could be measured to the hour does seem to suggest that he lived with owners who were equipped with a stopwatch and a gift for prophecy.

OLD CATS HOME

"… and cat food was only 10p a tin."

# 65 Celluloid dreams for swinging pussycats

Sixties cats make a bid for stardom on the silver screen

The 1960s was a vintage decade for cats at the movies. For years they had had to take a back seat while their witless canine contemporaries won filmgoers' hearts by barking, begging, rolling over or, in the case of Old Yeller, going to more extreme lengths by being shot for being rabid.

Four years after Old Yeller found himself staring up the wrong end of a rifle, cats capitalized on the spirit of sleek metropolitan cool that animated the new decade when one of their number starred opposite Audrey Hepburn's amoral socialite Holly Golightly in 1961's *Breakfast at Tiffany's*.

Holly's relationship with the cat mirrors how she feels about love. She refuses to name him, arguing that "I haven't got the right to give him one. We don't belong to each other."

The cat was played by a feline thespian known in real life as Orangey, and was reportedly so cantankerous that even veteran animal trainer Frank Inn didn't like him, but he did win a Patsy, the animal version of an Oscar.

"I'd just like to thank my trainer …"

Blofeld, the Bond villain, petted his first pampered Persian in 1963's *From Russia with Love*, but a more cuddly version of feline psychopathy was celebrated in the 1967 Disney film of *The Jungle Book*, in which the character Bagheera the panther is on hand to provide Mowgli with a wise, guiding paw.

The decade had space for another cat-centric film, 1965's *Faster Pussycat! Kill! Kill!* Directed by Russ Meyer, the pussycats were neither cartoons nor pets, but buxom homicidal strippers, and the line "You're a beautiful animal … I'm weak, and I want you" certainly wasn't a testimony to the joys of cat ownership.

# Smooth operator

Bilko the star but alley cat's theme tune strikes
a sewer note

"… his close friends get to call him 'TC', providing it's whipping for tea."

*Top Cat* was screened for the first time in 1961, detailing the
adventures of a gang and their leader, inspired by Phil Silvers as
Sergeant Bilko, but who, in a surreal twist, were all cats.

The cartoon's greatest mystery: what on earth its theme tune meant.
It cheerily told of "The most effectual Top Cat, whose intellectual
close friends get to call him TC", but the next line was lost by fitting
too many words into not enough tune.

Many seemed to think that it said "providing it's whacking the tee",
a seemingly random allusion to miscued golf shots, but thanks to the
glories of the internet, it can now be revealed that the garbled line
was "providing it's with dignity".

Wholly meaningless, but when you're watching a programme whose
star is a wisecracking cat in a boater and a waistcoat, there's really no
point quibbling over minor details.

# 67 Polydactyl cats toe the line

Big-footed beasts perfect pets for bear-like man of letters

Ernest Hemingway died in 1961. During his lifetime, he had considered the day wasted if it hadn't involved some terrible totemic battle between man and the elements, but the famously butch novelist had a gentler side.

Unlikely as it may sound, the author of such hard-bitten classics as *The Old Man and the Sea* and *Death in the Afternoon* loved cats. A sea captain gave him a polydactyl cat, a type of cat which has extra toes and is believed by some sailors to be a good luck charm, but his house on Key West provided home to many more.

Around 60 cats live at the Hemingway Home and Museum, half of them descended from the original polydactyl. Some carry the names of famous people, so it's the only place where you'll get to stroke Spencer Tracy or see Ava Gardner squatting behind a bush.

Great books he never wrote.

# Le chat est dans le stratosphère

Capsule cat rockets to a Gallic first

The Russians and Americans spent vast amounts of time and effort launching monkeys and dogs into space, but in 1963 the French demonstrated a typical Gallic insistence on doing things their own way by launching the first cat into space from the Colomb Becar rocket base in Algeria.

Just how extensively French the whole project was can be judged by the name of the rocket used in the launch. It was called Véronique. NASA had given their rockets classical names like Gemini and Apollo, the Russians were keen on turgid allusions to comradeship and Motherland, but only the French would give theirs the name of a beautiful woman.

It would be nice to imagine that, as Véronique soared upwards, a beret-wearing engineer exclaimed "zut alors" in wonderment, but perhaps not. In any case, at the centre of it all was a cat called Felix. Where other countries had carefully selected and trained their

animals, the French simply rounded up 14 stray cats from the streets of Paris and trusted to luck.

Felix was the one of the 14 selected for the famous flight and, safely installed in the capsule on top of Véronique, she completed her journey from obscurity by being rocketed to stardom. Or, more correctly, an altitude of 136 miles.

The sub-orbital flight was a success, particularly for Felix, who parachuted safely back to earth and straight into retirement. If you're wondering what happened to the other cats that had been selected, ten of them came up with a simple, but very feline, way of avoiding being fired into the ether. They ate so much during their training that they became too fat, and had to be discharged.

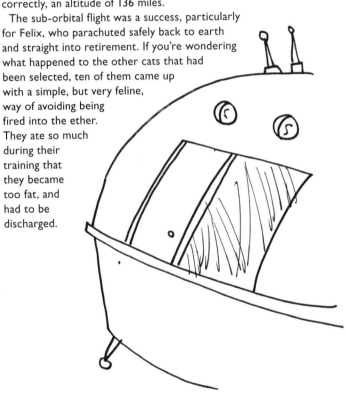

"Are you sure this is my new cat basket?"

# Narrator shares secret of the silent miaow

Classic cat book from a knockout sportswriter

A former sportswriter who was once knocked out by heavyweight champion Jack Dempsey, Paul Gallico reinvented himself as a novelist, writing gentle tearjerkers like *The Snow Goose* as well as a whole host of cat-centric fiction, including, in 1964, one of his best-loved books, *The Silent Miaow*.

Far from being the moving story of how a cat with laryngitis discovers sign language, *The Silent Miaow* is presented as "a manual for kittens, strays and homeless cats", supposedly written by a cat and then "translated from the Feline" by Gallico.

Turning conventional wisdom on its head, it describes how a cat should train its human family, although thankfully it avoids the vexed subject of toilet training. After all, there'd be nothing more unsettling than having to squat in a litter tray because the cat had retired to the bathroom with the paper.

"He wants us to use the litter tray?"

# The cat with the wandering paw

X-rated star with a swinging moral compass

Fritz the Cat was the cartoon animal for anyone who wondered if cartoon animals had a sex life. Striding where other characters had feared to tread, Fritz made a debauched and anarchic debut in *Help* magazine in 1965, starring in a story called "Fritz Comes on Strong".

Drawn by Robert Crumb, Fritz bore all the hallmarks of a creator who had been sexually fixated with Bugs Bunny as a teenager. Fully anthropomorphized and given an added dose of testosterone, Fritz gleefully does everything to anything and finally meets his end when he's stabbed in the head by a pneumatic female ostrich he's just sexually humiliated.

The animated version became the first cartoon to get an X-rating on its release in 1972, while Crumb's band, the Cheap Suit Serenaders, offered another feline-related assault on moral sensibilities with their faux-ragtime number "My Girl's Pussy", including the lines "I stroke it every chance I get; It's my girl's pussy."

# Full furry jacket

Cong go missing as cats snooze in heart of darkness

The story that the US Army used cats in the jungles of Vietnam during the late 1960s as a way of tracking the Viet Cong is possibly apocryphal, but that's no reason to avoid speculating on what shape the operations might have taken.

As music by the Doors plays in the background, the cats are sent out into the jungle in the dead of night, perhaps wearing small bandanas. They're summoned back just before dawn by a grizzled sergeant shouting "Frisky" and "Puss" while banging a fork against a bowl. The flaw in the plan becomes apparent only when the patrol leads soldiers not to the Viet Cong, but to a really nice place under a tree which is great for napping.

Still, it would have made a great scene for *Apocalypse Now*. As the choppers fly in supplies, Robert Duvall's character Lt Col Bill Kilgore takes a deep breath and remarks, "Ah, I love the smell of Whiskas in the morning."

The decision to use guide cats was not a success.

# LIKE A CAT ON A HOT TIN ROOF

# Pardon me, says lucky cat

Death row reprieve for cat who shot to stardom

In 1969, Morris the cat completed a journey which was the feline equivalent of Lincoln's progress from log cabin to White House when he went from a Chicago animal shelter to the forefront of Purina's Nine Lives cat food campaign.

The handsome orange tabby was rescued from the shelter by Bob Martwick, a professional animal trainer. Martwick's employers, the Leo Burnett advertising agency, fashioned the biddable cat into the furry face of Nine Lives, the premise being that he was simply too picky to eat anything else. They named him Morris and the rest was history.

Morris' fame was such that he was given a bodyguard to foil possible kidnap attempts. In 1974 he was the subject of *Morris: An Intimate Biography*, and even his death in 1978 failed to halt the steady advance of his career.

A successor was found from another shelter, one of a number of future Morrises who would go on to be garlanded with awards including the feline Oscar, known as the Patsy, and even to run for president in 1988 and 1992. Worryingly for the Democrats, Morris is said to have had better name recognition than anyone except President Bush.

None of them could beat the meteoric rise to stardom of the original Morris, which becomes particularly dramatic if you believe the reports which say he was 20 minutes from being destroyed when Bob Martwick rescued him – although Morris himself may not have been too surprised. His original name? Lucky.

MORRIS

# Litany of success
Cat's name is legion for her kittens are many

If you're going to be in the news, you may as well have a newsworthy name, and the four-year-old Burmese who bore the largest-ever recorded litter in August 1970 had a name that could easily grace the pages of the glossiest celebrity magazine. Step forward, Tarawood Antigone.

The cat with the five-star name was owned by Mrs Valerie Gane of Oxfordshire and her record-breaking litter had to be delivered by Caesarean. Four kittens were stillborn, but one female and 14 males survived, making a total of 19 kittens and, presumably, a very bewildered mother.

Tarawood Antigone retreated gracefully back into obscurity, while the proud father, who was half-Siamese, got ready to stand everyone down at the cattery a very large round indeed.

# Cats away
Enchanted Andy survives a pavement plunge

History tells of many dramatic feline escapes, but one death-defying cat merits a special mention here, as well as in the list of Guinness World Records – Andy, the amazing falling cat.

Andy belonged to Senator Ken Myer of Florida during the 1970s, and he still holds the record for the longest non-lethal fall, having survived an unplanned descent from the 16th floor of an apartment block, a drop of around 200 feet.

The cat could count himself fortunate to escape with eight of his nine lives, and the senator must have reflected that he was within a couple of feet of losing his furry companion, but an even greater mystery at the heart of the story remains unaddressed. Who calls a cat Andy?

# Hello Kitty, goodbye heart

Lovable cartoon cat laps up the adoration

The revolution, it's often said, will be televised. This is wrong. The revolution will not be televised. It will appear on stationery, spangly coin purses and unfeasibly sweet soft toys, and it will have an outsize cartoon cat's head. The movement shall be known by two words – "Hello Kitty".

Hello Kitty was created in 1974 by designer Ikuko Shimizu, who was working for Sanrio Co., a Japanese company which styles itself as a "social communication" business, which would seem to mean that it makes the kind of gifts, greetings cards and stationery that make some people get very excited and very squeaky.

Even though Shimizu later left the company, Sanrio pressed on. Bearing in mind the fact that people seem to be hardwired to find babies and kittens endearing, the company knew that something which was part-baby, part-kitten would have an effect similar to powerful pharmaceuticals.

Sanrio now has an annual turnover of around $1 billion, employs a battalion of artists and designers and has a list of items that runs well into the thousands, with the unassuming cartoon cat at the heart of it all. Hello Kitty would probably stand a reasonable chance of becoming prime minister of Japan if she could spend enough time away from being generally lovely to hit the campaign trail.

It would be easy to characterize

Hello Kitty, with its minimalist facial expression, as being the blank, emotionless stare of a world disappearing in a blizzard of trivia and scented notelets, but there's more to the cat than meets the eye.

Hello Kitty has not wasted her vice-like hold on the emotions, and has used it to raise thousands of dollars for UNICEF, so successfully that she has received the accolade "UNICEF Special Friend of Children". The future feline revolution might tend towards the cutesy, but at least its heart will be in the right place.

# 76 Lumpen Custard

Roobarb sees cartoon cat turn over a new leaf

*Roobarb* was shown for the first time on British TV in 1974. A cartoon series that detailed the adventures of Roobarb, a cheerily upbeat mongrel, it just wouldn't have been the same without Custard, the sarcastic purple cat who mocked his every endeavour from the safety of the garden fence.

A typically edgy British cartoon, it eschewed slick production values for erratic colours, wobbly lines, a maniacal theme tune and a general air of surrealistic anarchy that seemed like a lurid rebuke to the canned laughter and assembly-line ethos behind some of the Hanna-Barbera cartoons of the time.

The cartoon was repeated regularly over the next 15 years, and when it was resurrected with 39 new stories in 2005 the new series was named *Roobarb and Custard*, confirming Custard's position in the pantheon of great comedy cats.

The first *Roobarb and Custard* cartoon lacked excitement.

# Distillery cat becomes queen of the mousers

Tippling tortoiseshell calls time on reckless rodents

Some cats are content to doze away the days on a sunlit windowsill, but others have to work for a living, and none of them has worked harder than Towser, whose prowess as a mouser won her a Guinness World Record.

Towser caught a record-breaking 28,899 mice during her 24-year career at the Glenturret Distillery in Perthshire, Scotland, turning the country's oldest working Scotch whisky distillery and home of the "Famous Grouse" brand into an

address of infamy for any Scottish rodents seeking the distillery's supply of barley.

The modest tortoiseshell was finally called to the great distillery in the sky in 1987, although her statue still broods over her old patch, acting as warning to any errant mice.

Staff at Glenturret deny that Towser's secret was a dash of whisky in her nightly milk, and the present cat, Brooke, is remaining silent.

# 78 Moggy, moggy, moggy

Four-footed activist seeks union representation

Unions were often in the news during the 1980s, and from the same decade comes the story of Smudge, the cat who joined the ranks of the General, Municipal and Boilermakers' trade union.

Smudge worked as the resident mouser at the People's Palace, a museum and a massive glasshouse in Glasgow, ensuring that the people's experience of their local history wasn't marred by the people's mice scuttling around the people's corridors. Staff applied to NALGO for membership on Smudge's behalf; the cat was turned down but had better luck with the GMB.

The cat caused a local outcry by disappearing briefly in 1987, sauntering back a few weeks later – perhaps a temporary breakdown of relations caused Smudge to vote with its paws in Britain's first and only feline strike.

# Mothers in the mist

Maternally minded gorilla's heart is All Ball

What do you buy a captive gorilla for its birthday? Bananas would be passé and David Attenborough videos of gorillas in the wild might be thought of as tactless. Trainer Dr Francine Patterson asked Koko the gorilla what she wanted for her 12th birthday in 1984, and received a surprising answer. A cat.

Koko had been taught sign language, and signed the word for "cat", choosing a Manx kitten. It might have sounded like an episode of *Animal Hospital* waiting to happen, but the gorilla made an unexpectedly good mother. She doted on the cat, naming it All Ball, until tragedy intervened when the cat was run over and killed after getting out of Koko's enclosure.

All Ball was eventually replaced, but not before Koko used the sign language symbols for "cry" and "sad" to tell her trainer how she was feeling – and, she might have added, "in future, close the bloody cage properly".

# Shout it loud, be spangled and proud

Conservation-minded cat wears its heart on its sleeve

It's hard to think of a more patriotic-sounding cat than the California Spangled Cat, whose very name carries the image of a feline paean to the glories of the national flag of the United States of America and the republic for which it stands. But this is a cat with an altogether different story.

The distinctive California Spangled Cat was bred by Paul Casey in 1986, not to draw comparisons with the flag, but to draw attention to the plight of endangered cat species. The ultra-rare, spotted breed made its debut in the swish Neiman Marcus catalogue in a blaze of publicity, and with a suitably high price tag.

Numbers are limited, the waiting lists are long and California Spangled Cats often sell for thousands of dollars, so if you want to save endangered cats, it may be easier to donate direct to charity. Or buy the real thing.

# Bucking the cistern

Cat flush with success living in toilet

Cats have an unerring knack of finding sympathetic humans in even the most unlikely places, and so it was that in 1970 a stray six-month-old kitten was taken in by June Watson, who worked as an attendant in the toilets at Paddington station, where the cat made his home until 1983.

He became a celebrity, but fame had its price. The cat was brought tidbits by doting admirers who were so zealous in their devotion that, by 1982, he was named "London Fat Cat Champion", tipping the scales at 13.6 kg. But then he had to be put to sleep after vets found fluid in his lungs, a result of his excessive weight.

The poor cat had been spoilt to death, an accidental case of animal cruelty and a warning to other over-indulgent owners, although his name does still raise a smile. Well, what would you call a cat that lived in a toilet other than Tiddles?

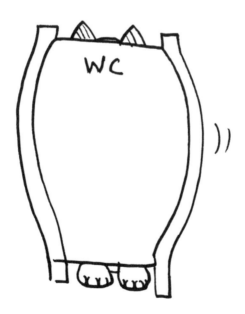

# Lucky dip

Arthur winkles his way to stardom with dextrous paws

"He doesn't get out of his basket for less than $1 million."

Cats have few aspirations beyond eating, sleeping and owning an eternally clean litter tray, but even the most modest moggy might have to concede that having a cat food named after you would carry a certain cachet. And that's exactly what happened to a white cat called Arthur in 1990.

Back in the 1960s when commercial television was introducing the idea of the ad-break to the Great British public, an earlier incarnation of Arthur had become famous as the Kattomeat cat. Arthur had a talent for winkling succulent meaty chunks out of the can with his paw, a simple trick which so impressed Spillers, who made Kattomeat, that they bought Arthur from his owner.

A public still getting used to the strange magic of television and mad

for novelty made Arthur a star and put Kattomeat on the map. The original Arthur died in 1976 and was replaced only a decade later, but by 1990 the Kattomeat brand was in the doghouse as young upstarts snatched away its sales.

The answer was to do away with the name, and replace it with the name of its most famous advocate, and so it was that "Arthur's" was launched in 1990, and yet another Arthur shot to stardom. Eleven commercials were made over the following four years, including one which saw the cat appearing with Dudley Moore, who had starred in the *Arthur* films.

Sales went up 21 per cent between 1991 and 1993, and, more importantly for Arthur, he managed to avoid the fate of an earlier namesake who added a new interpretation to the term "catnapping" when he was stolen. He was returned safely to Spillers a few days later, appetite for fame and Kattomeat undiminished.

# Armchair armageddon

Comedic cudgel better than rapier wit for duo with point to prove

Having a cartoon within a cartoon sounds like an achingly dull exercise in post-modern irony, but when the main cartoon in question is *The Simpsons* and the sub-cartoon is the splendidly dark "Itchy and Scratchy", it pays to bend the rules.

"Itchy and Scratchy" made their debut in the first series of *The Simpsons* in 1990, and are the cat and mouse stars of a cartoon popular with the Simpson children, Lisa and Bart. Used as a vehicle for typically pointed satire, the violence in "Itchy and Scratchy" is taken to excess and the laughter of the juvenile audience as blood spurts from every severed limb makes a neat point about violence-as-comedy.

The cartoon also gives *The Simpsons* creator Matt Groening the opportunity to send up some of the conventions in other cartoons, not least when a hip young dog called "Poochy" is clumsily introduced to give Itchy and Scratchy more youth appeal – a situation horribly familiar to anyone who has ever seen Scrappy-Doo.

"Itchy and Scratchy": the final season.

# 84 Fishy tail

Mousehole Cat tells the tall story of a valiant voyage

Antonia Barber's *The Mousehole Cat* was first published in 1990. The story tells of Tom, an old fisherman from the Cornish fishing village of Mousehole, who braves stormy seas to catch fish for his village, but the real star is Mowzer, Tom's magical cat.

Mowzer calms the Great Storm-Cat with her singing, and Tom's little boat arrives safely back at Mousehole with a full catch. The story is based on a Cornish folk tale about elderly fisherman Tom Bawcock, and the village celebrates

Tom Bawcock's Eve every December 23.

At the heart of the celebrations is Stargazy Pie, a fish pie which has fish heads poking though the pastry. Looking your dinner in the eye might not be everyone's cup of tea, but if you're partial to seafood – or you're a Mousehole cat – it's a unique way to experience the catch of the day.

# 85 Beam me up, Spotty

Enterprising cat with identity issues

The future according to *Star Trek* is a reassuring place. Admittedly, it may be peopled with actors who have been painted green and others who appear to have had a plastic baboon's bottom glued to their heads, but everybody looks fairly human. And they have cats.

"Someone's left a dead mouse on the transporter again."

A ginger cat wittily named Spot made his debut in the episode "Data's Day", in 1991, a part of the *Star Trek: the Next Generation* series, as the pet of Data, a member of the crew played by the aforementioned green-painted actor, Brent Spiner.

Spot starts out in the series as a long-haired male cat, becomes a short-haired cat and then gives birth to kittens, suggesting that someone in the continuity department may have been having a bit of an off-day.

The paradox is explained away with the tongue-in-cheek claim that Spot is a "shape shifter", a theory which gains credence in the episode in which Spot boldly goes where no cat has gone before and turns into an iguana.

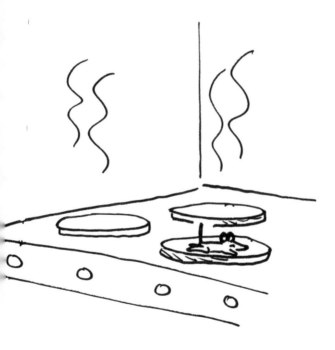

# Socks is shooed

Undiplomatic cat pays price for spurning buddy

For the duration of the Clinton administration, a cat called Socks had the honour of being First Cat.

A dapper black and white cat, Socks belonged to Chelsea Clinton's piano teacher before being offered a new home by the Clinton family, a home which would later become 1600 Pennsylvania Avenue, aka the White House, when Big Bill won the race for the presidency in 1992.

While Bill endured a torrid time over his dealings with a certain Ms Lewinsky, Socks was similarly stunned when the Clintons acquired a Labrador called Buddy. The two pets brawled on the South Lawn at the White House, and when the Clintons left in 2001 Socks was given to secretary Betty Currie.

As Bill later observed, "I did better with the Palestinians and the Israelis than I've done with Socks and Buddy."

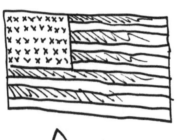

"I did NOT have sexual relations with that tabby."

# The furry civil servant

Cat who came in from the cold basks in the limelight

"The corridors of power" is a phrase often used by political pundits to describe the buildings where government goes about its business, but people seldom consider the staff who keep those corridors clean. Or, in the case of Humphrey, mouse-free.

As the Downing Street cat, Humphrey patrolled Britain's most famous address after being taken in as a stray by a civil servant. He drew a salary of £100 a year and served three prime ministers, and although he voted with his paws and left while John Major was in power, he soon returned.

By 1997, Humphrey was Chief Mouser to the Cabinet Office, but he disappeared from Number 10 amid rumours of policy differences with Mrs Blair. Questions were asked in the House about his welfare, and one newspaper invoked the Freedom of Information Act to find out where he'd gone, but Humphrey was happy living in obscurity, the one occupant of Downing Street able to make a dignified exit.

# Outback and out of order

Call for cull as outlaw cats massacre marsupials

Cats have a habit of making themselves at home no matter where they live, whether it's a house, a flat or the continent of Australia, where their habit of decimating indigenous wildlife such as the Bush-Tailed Bettong and the Eastern Barred Bandicoot led an Australian politician to call for a cat cull in 1996.

Richard Evans intervened on behalf of the Bettong, the Bandicoot and the Bilby, arguing that these native animals were being pushed to the brink of extinction by the three million-strong Australian pet cat population's unfortunate habit of eating them.

Evans called for "the total eradication of cats in Australia by 2020", and asked scientists to release a fatal virus to kill them, but failed to explain how the virus would tell a native marsupial from a cat. Stories that cats have called for the total eradication of Richard Evans remain unsubstantiated.

The cats got their revenge in first.

# 89 Furry rider

Rastus and Max ride the road to eternity

People often say that some cats and their owners are inseparable, but Max Corkhill and his cat Rastus were arguably the closest – and most distinctive – human and cat companions of all time.

Corkhill was a biker, and found Rastus, deserted, at a bike meet. The pair travelled miles around Corkhill's native New Zealand together, raising money for the Society for the Prevention of Cruelty to Animals. Rastus, a handsome black Bombay cross, perched on the bearded biker's petrol tank or handlebars, and, like Corkhill, sported its own red bandana and a custom-made helmet.

Rastus was killed in 1998 in a head-on crash that also claimed the life of Corkhill's partner and pillion passenger, Gaynor Martin. He and Rastus had lived together, died together, and were cremated together, with 1,000 bikers following the funeral procession to escort them on their last journey.

# Yes, fur minister

Feline not for turning as Cat Mandu leads the loonies

Following the death of their leader Screaming Lord Sutch, the Official Monster Raving Loony Party did what any party worth the name would do. They held a leadership election, and promptly voted in a cat as the joint leader, alongside a man who rejoices in the name Alan "Howling Laud" Hope.

By comparison, Cat Mandu was a positively sensible name for a cat, if not for the leader of a political party, no matter how officially loony it is, but the ginger tomcat swept to power at the 1999 party conference, held at Howling Laud Hope's hotel in Devon.

*Cat World* tracked him down for an interview, and were told that the new leader liked to eat "Meaty Chunks from the cash and carry" and had spent several days stuck in a gulley on the hotel roof, not a predicament often associated with senior politicians.

Pictures taken at the launch of the party's manifesto for the 2001 General Election – a blank sheet

"The PM's just coughing up a hairball."

of paper – showed Cat Mandu as a cat whose peeved expression may have been something to do with the fact that it was sporting a small felt top hat, a rosette and possibly longing for a quiet life back up on the roof.

The party polled well, but Cat Mandu was killed in a road accident the following year, marking the end of the party's flirtation with four-footed politicians. But perhaps it's not the end of cats' ambitions.

Past loony policies have been the abolition of the 11-plus, all-day licensing hours and pet passports, all of which are now law, so the day may yet come when a tabby and a tortoiseshell are staring each other out at the despatch box, going all fluffy and making strange caterwauling noises.

# Hairless whisper

Inscrutable Sphynx needs the gentle touch

As hairless as it is alarming, the Sphynx is one of the most unusual breeds of cat. Sphynx cats generally lack fur and whiskers and, although some are covered in a fine, downy fur, their general appearance is of a cat that is waiting for its coat to come out of the tumble dryer.

The story of the breed begins in 1966 when a cat gave birth to a hairless kitten, as a result of a bizarre but entirely natural genetic mutation. Where many people see an ugly cat, the cat breeders see a business opportunity, and a new breed, now known as the Sphynx, soon came into being.

Sphynx cats shot to stardom when a Sphynx played Dr Evil's cat in the Austin Powers sequel, 1999's *The Spy Who Shagged Me*. The cat's real name? Mel Gibskin or Ted Nudegent, depending on which website you believe.

# Sixty paws a minute

Applying PawSense results in Ig Nobel reward

"He's playing Minesweeper again."

The Ig Nobel Prize is awarded for magnificently pointless scientific achievements which, in the words of founder and science journalist Marc Abrahams, "cannot or should not be reproduced". Past winners have included studies of the trajectory of penguin faeces, activity in the brains of locusts watching *Star Wars*, and a piece of software called PawSense.

PawSense won Chris Niswander from Tucson, Arizona, an Ig Nobel Prize in the computer science category in 2000. Niswander's software recognizes the kind of random keystrokes produced when a cat is walking along a computer keyboard and locks the keys, as well as producing a noise to drive the cat away.

As valuable as PawSense is, it's unlikely that Niswander had as much fun creating it as the winners of the medical category. Their study? "Magnetic Resonance Imaging of Male and Female Genitals During Coitus and Female Sexual Arousal".

**Romulus, Remus ... and Puss**

Cats build a lasting colony at the heart of the eternal city

The spread of cats around Europe and, eventually, the world began when they were adopted as in-house pest controllers by the Romans, so it's only fitting that Rome should be the unofficial feral cat capital of the world.

Some estimates suggest that there are as many as 300,000 feral cats living in the Italian capital, and in 2001 the city decided to give legal protection to the cats lazing languidly in the ruins of the Coliseum, the Forum and at Torre Argentina, on the grounds that they represent part of Rome's bio-heritage.

Women known as "gattare" – literally "cat women" in Italian – help to look after the cats as does an organization known as the Friends of Roman Cats. A cat sanctuary is based at Torre Argentina, and the cats may have gained a very influential advocate indeed – Pope Benedict.

# Wanted posters

Docket boosts sales as artwork vanishes

"It's her most challenging work."

When Tracy Emin's cat, Docket, went missing in 2002, the young British artist did what any other cat owner would do and put up a series of "missing" posters to alert people to the plight of the errant feline.

The problem is that when you're a former Turner Prize nominee who shot to fame through a series of esoteric artworks that used subject matter as disparate as a bed and a tent bearing the name of anyone you've ever slept with, people might think that your cat posters are just an extravagant visual gag. Or just a chance to own some Emin. Whatever the reason, collectors took them down as fast as Emin could put them up.

Emin was genuinely upset, but it didn't stop the disappearing posters being valued at around £500 each. Fortunately, Docket returned home safely, while the kind of people who would feel the need to spend three-figure sums on a torn-down poster went back to their crushingly pointless lives.

# Back to black

Scientists probe lucky genetic inheritance

Scientists seem to spend a disproportionate amount of time on substantially irrelevant pieces of research. And back in 2003, said scientists were busily working out whether or not black cats really are lucky.

Carried out by scientists at the National Cancer Institute and the University of Maryland in the US, the research did have a point, as it was designed to work out whether the gene for black fur was linked to an ability to resist disease, which would have implications for humans.

The black cat was a lucky symbol long before science got involved, and is still used as a lucky logo by companies, organizations and sports clubs, including Sunderland FC, whose nickname is the "Black Cats". Sunderland disproved the lucky hypothesis by getting relegated from the Premiership in 2006 with the wholly unlucky tally of 15 points.

# Hammer time

Private matter becomes public knowledge as cat comes home

When his unit was serving in Iraq, Staff Sergeant Rick Bousfield's unit picked up an extra member in 2003 – a cat called Private Hammer.

The distinctive tiger-striped cat found its way into their tents and was soon adopted as both a mouser and a mascot. When it was time for the unit to return home, leaving Private Hammer behind, the Staff Sergeant wrote to Alley Cat Allies, a Washington DC-based non-profit organization specializing in feral cats.

His heart-rending plea was as follows: "We consider him one of our troops. If there was a way that ACA could help get Hammer back to the States it would be a wonderful boost for the men to see the cat who has won their hearts free."

It proved impossible to resist. Hammer now lives happily with Bousfield and his family, but the reaction of the other five cats in his household is harder to gauge.

# Copycat becomes latest development

Modest deposit guarantees owner's personal clone

The loss of a cat is a bitter blow for any cat owner. Some find another cat, and sometimes another cat finds them, but when a 17-year-old Maine Coon called Nicky died in 2003, his owner decided to call on the services of a Californian company called Genetic Savings and Clone, a name that should give you some idea as to what happened next.

The company offers what it refers to as "gene banking and cloning of exceptional pets". Using DNA from Nicky, it delivered the first commercially cloned cat in December 2004. This perfect copy of the original was named Little Nicky in his honour, and his owner appeared on *Good Morning America* to tell the world how pleased she was with the results.

"He looks identical," she said. "His personality is extremely similar; they

are very close." But the fact that she had asked to be identified only as "Julie" suggested that some people were unhappy with her decision.

Little Nicky had cost Julie $50,000, and as an academic from Stanford University's Center for Biomedical Ethics told the BBC, "For $50,000, she could have provided homes for a lot of strays."

Yet by the time the story broke, Genetic Savings and Clone already had orders for five more cloned cats and can now proudly call itself "the leading provider of pet gene banking and pet cloning services".

Concerns about the ethics of cloning still exist, but any company which has the sense to cover its website with pictures of doe-eyed little kittens longing to be loved would probably be a tough place to close down.

# Supersize cat
Leo goes large but Peebles is a half-pint

Cats come in all shapes and sizes and nothing illustrates that variety better than a brief look at Leo and his diminutive counterpart, Mr Peebles.

Leo sits at one end of the great, figurative see-saw of cat sizes. A Maine Coon, Leo is the largest of a naturally large breed, measuring 48 inches from his nose to the tip of his tail, making him the world's longest cat, as the judges for Guinness World Records don't recognize the "biggest cat" category, believing that it might encourage overfeeding.

At the other end of the see-saw sits Mr Peebles, albeit much, much higher in the air. Young Mr Peebles has a genetic defect which stops him from growing, and he became a Guinness World Record holder in 2004 as officially the world's smallest cat, measuring just 6 inches high.

Mr Peebles weighs 3 lbs to Leo's 35 lbs, a profound difference in weight and, presumably, in cat food bills.

**Purrfect pint**

Kippered cat rolls out the barrel

Beer is not a drink commonly associated with cats, who, given a choice, would prefer some milk, or perhaps some rancid water from next door's fish pond, but in 2005 the Castle Rock Brewery in Nottingham began brewing a beer in honour of a local pub cat.

The brewery sells its frothy wares through the Vat and Fiddle pub next door, a pub which is also home to Kipper, a black and white female cat who had wandered in nine years before and ignored shouts of last orders ever since.

When Kipper needed medical attention, the brewery came up with the bright idea of brewing a special beer to help pay the fees, and "Castle Rock Kipper" duly went on sale. It might not sound like the most appealing pint around, but it's said to be a rich, tasty brew, and when you're asked why you're going to the bar, you can always say that you're going to drink one more for the Kipper.

To avoid capture, British big cats move with the times.

Britain is a strange and ancient country, wreathed in mists and mystery. Some people tell of a demonic dog called Black Shuck who once roamed East Anglia, but while Shuck is the stuff of legend, a growing number of big cat sightings suggest that the hound has some very real competition.

The first British Big Cats Conference was held in 2006 and, according to the British Big Cat Society (BBCS), there were 2,123 sightings of big cats between April 2004 and July 2005, many involving large black cats. The skull of a lynx was recovered in Devon in 2005 and large paw-prints suggest that there may be more substance to the sightings than a few too many pints of scrumpy.

What big cats really need to make headlines, though, is a catchy nickname. The mysterious feline predators are best served with lurid names like "The Beast of Bodmin Moor" and "The Terror of Trellech", so pity the puma-like beast caught on a CCTV camera in 1999. Its name? "The Telford Puma".

# Molly's alone

New York cat crawls through spaces broad and narrow

New Yorkers know what they want, and how to get it. Capital city of customer service, it's a place where serving a tall skinny mocha latte that isn't quite tall or skinny enough is seen as an incitement to violence. So when a cat called Molly got stuck in the bowels of a Greenwich Village deli in April 2006, there was no way that the denizens of the Big Apple were going to give up on her.

When the cat disappeared into the walls the deli, owner Peter Myer consulted the usual authorities, but it became obvious that Molly wasn't going to budge. This being New York, the rescuers turned to less conventional means.

A cat therapist was called in to play whale noises to the cat, a cat psychic was summoned to commune with her on a higher plane, and a litter of mewing kittens was used in a doomed attempt to appeal to Molly's latent maternal instincts. But after two weeks, she was still lost to the outside world.

And then Kevin Clifford got involved with the rescue effort. A tunnel worker, Kevin brought the tools of his trade to bear on the fabric of the deli, hoping that brute force and a power drill would succeed where whales and kittens had failed.

Four hours and a large amount of brick and plaster later, Molly was free, and found to be suffering from nothing more serious than dehydration, said by one reporter to be a testament to the fortifying powers of finger food.

"It's no good – fetch that tom from next door."

# THE CAT THAT GOT THE CREAM